YOUR KNOWLEDGE HAS VALUE

Bibliographic information published by the German National Library:

The German National Library lists this publication in the National Bibliography; detailed bibliographic data are available on the Internet at http://dnb.dnb.de .

Imprint:

Copyright © 2017 GRIN Verlag, Open Publishing GmbH
Print and binding: Books on Demand GmbH, Norderstedt Germany
ISBN: 9783668537460

This book at GRIN:

http://www.grin.com/en/e-book/373656/establishing-an-innovation-culture-at-general-mills-canada

Felix Zappe

Establishing an Innovation Culture at General Mills Canada

Based on the Ivey School's Case "General Mills Canada: Building a Culture of Innovation (B)"

GRIN Publishing

GRIN - Your knowledge has value

Since its foundation in 1998, GRIN has specialized in publishing academic texts by students, college teachers and other academics as e-book and printed book. The website www.grin.com is an ideal platform for presenting term papers, final papers, scientific essays, dissertations and specialist books.

Visit us on the internet:

http://www.grin.com/

http://www.facebook.com/grincom

http://www.twitter.com/grin_com

Establishing an Innovation Culture at
General Mills Canada

Based on the Ivey School's Case "General Mills Canada: Building a Culture of Innovation (B)"

Handed in by: **Felix Zappe**

Content

Tables and figures

1 Assessment of described efforts

An assessment of the described efforts of the change towards a more innovative company culture, it is important to look at the efforts taken from a holistic perspective. According to the case (Ken and Mitchell, 2014), the new innovation initiative, the 'culture of innovation'-programme, was based on three pillars and was introduced in accordance with the ideas and in consent with the whole leadership level. The three pillars described are 'Ask. Enable. Recognize.' And follow a road map based on the three pillars (see figure 1). Essential for this process, especially in the beginning, was a common definition of innovation and the process of developing a common understanding of the role and characteristics of innovation in the company, e.g. by the clarification of common misconceptions regarding innovation especially at General Mills Canada (GMC). This got contributed by the acquisition of a new brand of yoghurts that opened a lot of space for innovation and especially the for the hiring of new employees. Further measures described were the rearrangement of the company buildings to a more engaging, friendly and creativity and informal exchange fostering layout, the rearrangement of meeting routines, e.g. encouraging free Fridays and more flexible working times, ongoing training and encouragement sessions for and between employees. The HR department even organized an innovation team to take care on organizational aspects regarding all these matters, all to encourage employees to rise from analysis paralysis and towards a bigger and bolder style of tackling challenges. During this initiative the reward system for innovative behavior was renamed and slightly changed from 'thinking outside the box' towards an innovative and creative way of working.

While all these changes seem to reach managers partially, as some of them understand the new innovation approach of 'everything that makes GMC better' to the fullest, a large part of the employees and some of the managers don't seem to like it, as they don't approve some and even are confused about the measures. The company climate survey, a very direct measurement of the employees feelings, of 2012, the year of the start of the innovation initiative and with the most changes and spending regarding this topic, shows also almost no effect on the items that shall measure the perceived innovativeness within GMC's culture.

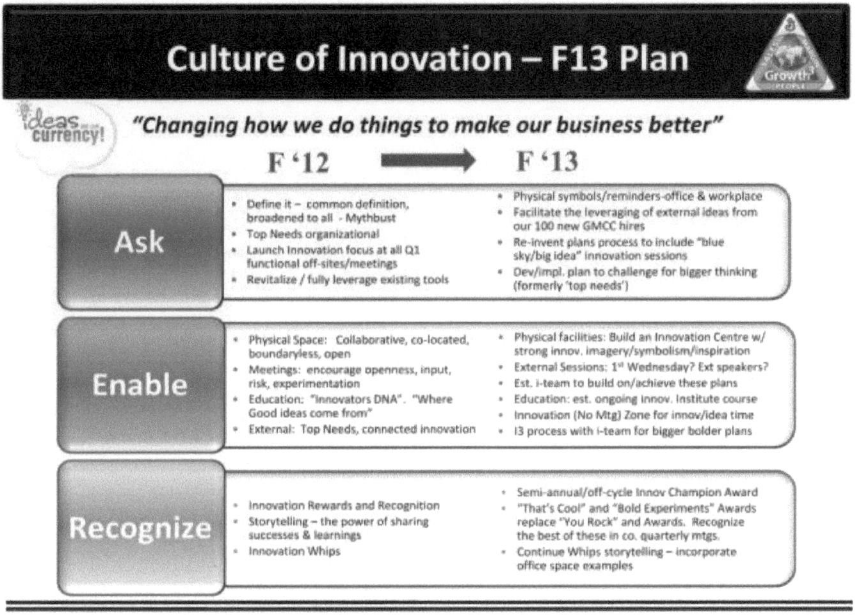

Figure 1: Culture of Innovation Road map (Source: Mark and Mitchell, 2014, p. 4).

The main points brought up by managers in regard of disproving the measures where:

- Not linking specific measures to the 'culture of innovation'-programme
- Feeling not encouraged enough towards a more innovative working behavior
- Inconsistent definitions and programmes regarding innovations at GMC
- Remaining short term profit orientation
- Hippocratic relation to the goal of innovativeness and the actual risks that will be taken
- Neglect of the core business and dilution of the actual business of GMC
- Neglect of external circumstances such as the general economy, competitors and emerging markets

In conclusion, the assessment of the described efforts of installing a culture of innovation through the 'culture of innovation'-programme at GMC must take in consideration the fundamental framework and it's elaboration on actual viable measures but also on the way it is backed up and understood throughout the company, which is influenced by the way it is presented, adopted and felt for the employees. In other words this can be described by the culture model of Schein and Schein (2016), which distinguish between 3 levels of a culture (see figure 2). In regard to this model the fundamental framework can be understood as the espoused value, the viable measures as the behavior and artefacts and the way it is backed up through the company are the basic assumptions.

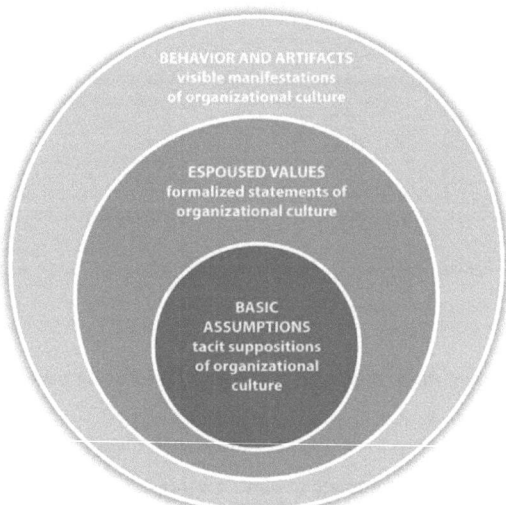

Figure 2: Schein-Model of culture (Source: Schein and Schein, 2016).

Homer and Taylor did a lot to elaborate their very sophisticated approach of an innovational culture into almost every part of the company on the level of behavior and artefacts, even came up with measures that didn't worked as planned and renewed them. Further they came up with follow up measures even for succeeding ones and had an approach of displaying espoused values through their framework. However all their efforts weren't backed up in the company by shared basic assumptions regarding innovation and its necessity, which prevented, as shown in figure 2, the targeted impact of level 2 and level 3 measures as their foundations were not given.

The final assessment must therefore be as follows: Homer and Taylor offered a very elaborated and thought through approach with a very sophisticated implementation but a lack in back up and foundation in the company and therefore somewhat without long-lasting impact.

2   Further ideas for cultural change

Further ideas for cultural change within the presented case should, regarding our conclusions in chapter 1 focus on establishing shared Basic Assumptions. An approach what these Basic Assumptions might be, is given on the one hand by the statements of the managers about what they think is currently out of place in the 'culture of innovation'-programme and on the other hand for the majority of employees by the model of 'four levers of influence' suggested by Keller & Price (2011, see figure 3).

In this model they argue that the key to influence the behavior and beliefs of persons can be changed by the following 4 levers:

- A compelling story, i.e. an understandable narrative reasoning the change
- Reinforcement mechanics, i.e. the feeling that a change is appreciated and possible within the given framework of the organization they are in
- Skills required for change, i.e. the certainty that the new way they are supposed to behave is within their skillset or they are given the possibility to evolve these skills
- Role modeling, i.e. the feeling that everybody around them is also behaving in the new, targeted way

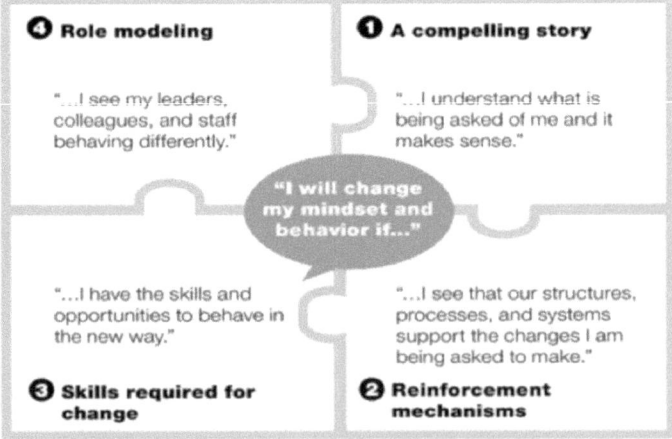

Figure 3: Four levers of influence (Source: Keller and Price, 2011).

Of course this is just one way to change the normative basic assumption of an organization, which also excludes people that are behaving naturally odd. Especially in the innovation context this could be a topic that deserves regards as these behaviors are often the sparks for inventions or creative input. However, even in a normatively as more creative environment perceived these people might find a way to behave according to their natural and regardless of this minority it is the perception of the majority that shapes the normative culture of an organization.

Regarding these two approaches further ideas fur cultural change are given as described in table 1 to foster the Basic Assumption of GMC's innovation approach and strengthen the existing and hopefully ongoing measures of the 'culture of innovation'-programme.

Table 1: Ideas to foster the Basic Assumptions of GMC's innovation approach (Source: Own depiction partially based on Keller and Price, 2011).

Managerial level	
Deficiency	**Counter-measure**
Not linking specific measures to the 'culture of innovation'-programme	• Clearly describing the 'culture of innovation'-programme as a whole to all managerial positions, including all parts of the framework and the road map
Feeling not encouraged enough towards a more innovative working behavior	• Making sure that individual managers match their position in terms of new upcoming tasks • Ensure suitable training or the adoption of new tasks • Making them aware for the measure of 3).
Inconsistent definitions and programmes regarding innovations at GMC	• Introducing the managers to one definition and sticking to it

	• Interlinking several measures under the introduced 'culture of innovation'-programme
Remaining short term profit orientation	• Linking innovative goals the GMC business plan and subsequently to the managers performance indexes
Hippocratic relation to the goal of innovativeness and the actual risks that will be taken	• Ensure full risk affinity as described in 3.
Neglect of the core business and dilution of the actual business of GMC	• Clear definition of the core businesses for each brand • Clear trend analysis and the definition of favorable scopes of action
Neglect of external circumstances such as the general economy, competitors and emerging markets	• Ongoing trend and environment analysis • Interlinking of strategic and innovative goals and measures accordingly
Employee level	
Lever of influence	**Measures**
A compelling story	• Event for all employees where the narrative for innovative is delivered and everybody is aligned under this goal • Consistent and transparent communication of the new goal
Reinforcement mechanics	• General guideline: Everybody is granted what he needs to function as best as he can, of course within boundaries of reasonability

	• Measures as described under 3. Especially regarding 'Rewards', 'Goals' and 'Risk-Taking'
Skills required	• Introduction of a budget for training or schooling per employee • Periodical check if job description and skills of the employee still match • Measures as described under 3. Especially regarding 'Tools', 'Knowledge' and 'Resources'
Role Modeling	• Direct conversation channels to the manager • Informal meetings such as a 'lunch roulette' with all colleagues • New routines are shown and lived by the managers, not in an authorial way but as the first among equals. • Measures as described under 3. Especially regarding 'Relationships'

3   Organizational support capabilities

To support the ideas given in chapter 2 the GMC on an organizational level has to contribute also, as especially made clear by the managerial statements and the lever of change 'rein-forcement mechanics'. How this despite the already described and implemented tools could work is described on an organizational level by Maher (2014) in the 'Dimensions of innova-tion culture'-model. In this model (see figure 4) Maher describes the seven dimensions of innovations has developed earlier with her colleagues.

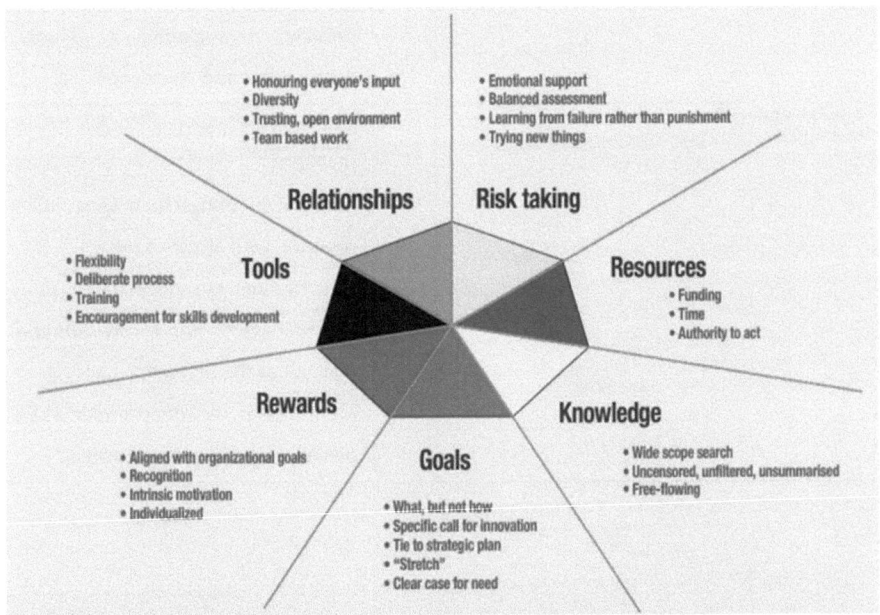

Figure 4: Dimensions of innovative culture (Source: Maher, 2014, p. 5).

Each of the seven dimensions has several directives, which function as guidelines, for what an organization has to provide in order to fully embrace the contribution of one dimension towards its innovative culture. These seven dimensions are:

- Risk-taking
- Resources
- Knowledge
- Goals

- Rewards
- Tools
- Relationship

Accordingly to Maher the dimension 'Risk-taking' has the directives of emotional support, balanced assessment, learning from failure rather than from punishment, trying new things.

These directives are to be translated very directly into recommendations for action, which are to be undertaken by GMC to intensify their culture of innovation. See a possible list of recommendations for action in table 2.

Table 2: Recommendations for actions for GMC on an organizational level (Source: Own depiction based on Maher, 2014, p.5).

Dimension	Directive	Recommendation
Risk-taking	Emotional support	• Colleagues and managers should have basics in positive psychology • No pressure policies • Psychological treatment is granted, sabbatical or other means are easily given
	Balanced assessment	• Risk assessment should use scenario technique and at least be done by two employees
	Learning from failure rather	• Embracing of failures

	than from punishment	should be learned
		• Everybody should be trained in acceptance and resilience
		• No punishments but the celebrations of failures
	Trying new things	• The organization should introduce slight, reasonable but tangible changes in structures or routines
		• Employees should reflect on their own ability to try new things
Resources	Funding	• The funding for a new project after reasonable assessment should be easily accessible, e.g. Through a dedicated budget
	Time	• Workloads are calculated with a time puffer
	Authority to act	• Employees should be given the competences to make their decisions

Knowledge	Wide scope search	• In the beginning of knowledge driven processes, all input is welcome
	Uncensored, unfiltered, not summarized	• Information about project are always open to everyone
	Free-flowing	• Knowledge transfer is embraced • Each competency should be at least twice in the company
Goals	What, but not how	• Openness to all approaches if a goal can be reached with it
	Specific call for innovation	• Goals and future plans should be communicated
	Tie to strategic plan	• The company strategy is clear, accessible to everyone and all sub-goals are derived from it
	"Stretch"	• Goals shall be challenging but not impossible
	Clear case for need	• Each need should underlie a use-case • Each use-case must be logic

		•
Rewards	Aligned with organizational goals	• Two parties are benefiting from the reward, the rewarded and the company
	Recognition	• Rewards and honors are being celebrated and openly visible • Everybody's contribution gets recognized
	Intrinsic motivation	• Rewards shall be provided according to the motivational structure of the rewarded
	Individualized	• Each employee can choose what he gets
Tools	Flexibility	• There are no teams but competencies • People are asked because of their competencies to join a project
	Deliberate process	• Processes underlie their specific goals
	Training	• Everybody is granted to earn, train or access for the skills he currently needs or

			will need
	Encouragement for skill development	•	Reasonable enquiries for skill development are very likely to be granted
Relationships	Honoring everyone's input	•	Meetings are open to anyone
		•	Focus on competences rather than hierarchy
	Diversity	•	Diversity should be introduced to team structures, not only ethnically but regarding life realities
	Trusting, open environment	•	Everybody speaks about problems, not persons
		•	'I can'- and 'you can'-attitude
	Team-based work	•	Every work should be checked according the 'two-man'-rule

References

Keller, S. and Price, C., 2011. *Beyond Performance: How Great Organizations Build Ultimate Competitive Advantage*. UK, USA: John Wiley and sons.

Maher, L., 2014. Building a culture for innovation: a leadership challenge. *World hospitals and health services: the official journal of the International Hospital Federation*, 50 (1), pp. 4-6.

Mark, K. and Mitchell, J. R., 2014. *General Mills Canada: Building a culture of Innovation (B)*. W14004 – Version 2014-01-30. Ivey Business School, Western University, London, Ontario, Canada: Ivey Publishing.

Schein, E. and Schein, P., 2016. *Organizational culture and leadership*. 5th ed. USA: John Wiley and sons.

YOUR KNOWLEDGE HAS VALUE